# A Kid's Guide to Drawing™

# How to Draw
# Sharks

Justin Lee

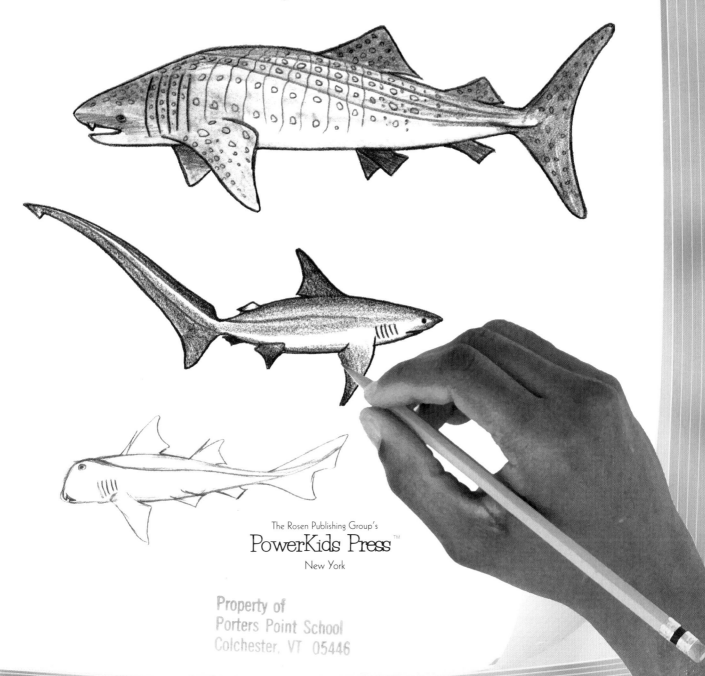

The Rosen Publishing Group's
PowerKids Press™
New York

For Cori, the world's coolest little brother

Published in 2002 by The Rosen Publishing Group, Inc.
29 East 21st Street, New York, NY 10010

First Edition

Book Design: Kim Sonsky
Layout: Michael Caroleo
Project Editor: Frances E. Ruffin

Photo Credits: pp. 10, 12, 18, 20 © Innerspace Visions; pp. 6, 8, 14, 16 © Digital Stock.

Lee, Justin, 1973–
    How to draw sharks / Justin Lee.—1st ed.
            p. cm. — (A kid's guide to drawing)
Includes index.
  ISBN 0-8239-5788-8 (lib. bdg.)
1. Sharks in art—Juvenile literature.  2. Drawing—Technique—Juvenile literature.  [1. Sharks in art.  2. Drawing—Technique.]  I. Title. II. Series.
  NC781 .L44 2002
  743.6'73—dc21

Manufactured in the United States of America

# CONTENTS

# Let's Draw Sharks

Drawing sharks can be fun! We have all heard stories about sharks killing people. Many **species** of shark, however, are not harmful to humans. There are more than 300 different species of sharks. You will learn how to draw eight different types of sharks. You will learn what and how they eat and how they swim.

Sharks belong to an ancient **class** of animals called Chondrichthyes. Their **ancestors** appeared on Earth 360 to 408 million years ago. Sharks have changed little over the last 100 million years. Many sharks are hunted or killed accidentally by fishermen. Some sharks are **endangered**. We must protect them. We can start by understanding them. Drawing sharks is a great way to learn about these amazing animals.

Here is a list of supplies that you will need for drawing sharks:

- A sketch pad
- A number 2 pencil
- A pencil sharpener
- An eraser

All of the shark drawings in this book begin with a simple shape, usually an oval. You will add other shapes such as circles, curved lines, and triangles. These are listed on page 22 as "drawing terms."

You can learn to draw each shark in several steps. It took millions of years for sharks to evolve into their shapes. Don't be upset if it takes you a few hours to learn to draw them. The more you practice, the better your drawings will be. Start drawing lightly and erase smudges. Keep drawing, and pretty soon your shark drawings will **evolve**!

# Great White Shark

The great white shark can be found in oceans around the world. The biggest great white shark ever caught was 23 feet (7 m) long and weighed more than 7,000 pounds (3,175 kg). White sharks are **predators**. They eat sea lions, seals, fish, dolphins, and other sharks. Like all sharks, white sharks have no bones. Their skeletons are made of cartilage, the same material that our noses and ears are made of. Great white sharks can swim about 15 miles (24.1 km) per hour. They have sharp teeth that they use to rip and slice their **prey**. Some sharks lose up to 30,000 teeth in their lifetime, and some sharks can replace a tooth in eight days.

1

Draw a long, flat oval. Add a box at one end for the head, and two lines tapering at the other end for the tail.

2

Add a mouth, teeth, an eye, a nostril, and gill openings.

3

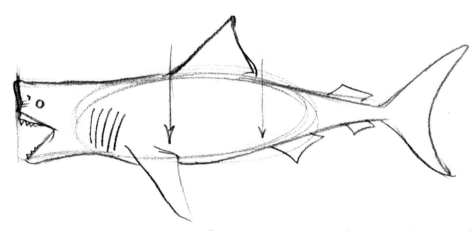

Next draw the triangle-shaped dorsal fin on top, behind the center of your oval. Draw the pectoral fin behind the gill openings.
Draw the pelvic fin. It lies below the back of the dorsal fin. Add the two other small fins. Now draw the tail.

4

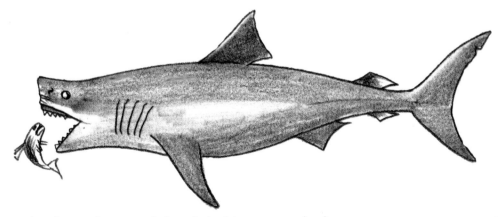

Add shading. Make the outlines and details bolder. Erase the lines you don't need.

7

# Shortfin Mako Shark

The shortfin mako shark is the fastest shark, reaching speeds of up to 20 miles per hour (32.2 km/h). Adults can be from 10 to 13 feet (3 to 4 m) long and weigh more than 1,000 pounds (454 kg). People all over the world eat this shark. All this fishing and hunting endangers the mako shark. Some scientists think there are less than half as many shortfins now as there were in 1978. Some sharks have babies by laying eggs. Shortfin mako sharks give birth to 8 or as many as 10 live shark pups. These baby sharks are born ready to hunt for themselves.

**1**

Start with a pointed oval. Draw two triangles for the tail. Remember to draw the top one bigger.

**2**

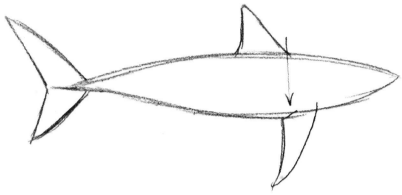

Next draw the dorsal fin above the middle of the oval.
The back of the pectoral fin lines up with the front of the dorsal fin. Draw it.

**3**

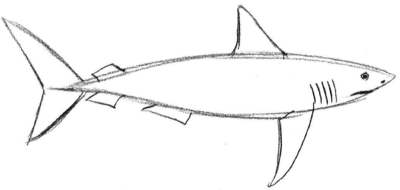

Add gill openings, an eye, a nostril, a mouth, and other fins.

**4**

Add shading. Sharpen details. (Did you catch the notch in the tail?)
Clean up with your eraser.

# Thresher Shark

The thresher shark's tail is nearly as long as its body. Thresher sharks live near the surface of the ocean. They use their tails to build up a lot of speed and jump completely out of the water. Thresher sharks can grow to be 13 feet (4 m) long and can weigh up to 1,000 pounds (454 kg). They eat fish, squid, octopus, other sharks, and even birds. Threshers use their long tails to herd schools of fish into tight groups. They swim around the fish in smaller and smaller circles. When the fish are all bunched up, the thresher swims through the group of fish, eating as quickly as it can.

1

Draw an oval with pointed ends. Add the tail. Make it as long as the body.

2

Add the dorsal fin above the middle of the body.
Carefully look at the top and bottom part of the tail. Now draw them, lightly at first.

3

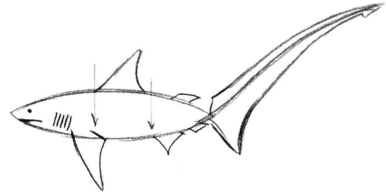

Add the other fins and details. Pay close attention and add the right details to the right places.

4

Add shading. Sharpen lines and details. Clean up any smudges with your eraser. You've drawn a cool-looking shark!

# Sand Tiger Shark

Sand tiger sharks have teeth that curve backward. Any unlucky fish caught inside a sand tiger's mouth can't escape. The curved teeth are good for keeping fish in, but they aren't very good for biting and chewing. Sand tiger sharks swallow their food whole. It may take several days for them to digest a meal. Sand tiger sharks grow to be from 10 to 14 feet (3 to 4.3 m) long. Few sharks float in the water. If they stop swimming, they sink. Sand tigers have found a way to solve that problem. They swim to the surface and swallow a mouthful of air. The air in their stomachs keeps them floating in the water.

Draw a long, flat oval with an extending point at one end for the head, and a long, bending point at the other end for the tail.

2

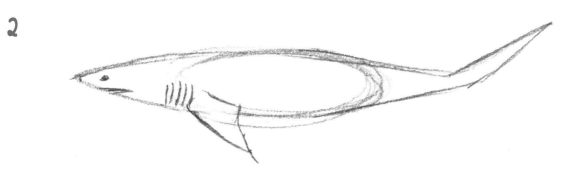

Draw the mouth and eye. Add gill openings and a pectoral fin.

3

Look at the tail fin. Draw it, lightly at first. Add the other fins, which should be about the same size.

4

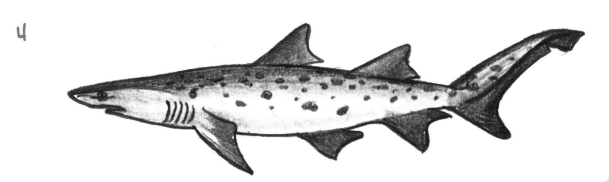

Add shading. Sharpen outlines and details. Clean up any smudges with your eraser.

# Hammerhead Shark

The hammerhead is one of the most unusual-looking animals in the sea. Its head is shaped like a long bar with eyes on either end. There are several different types of hammerhead sharks. You are going to draw the great hammerhead. The great hammerhead is large and aggressive, growing to almost 20 feet (6.1 m). Its wedge-shaped head acts as a **rudder**, making the hammerhead a very good swimmer. Because its eyes are on each side of its head, the hammerhead can see better than most sharks. Sharks have a sense that we don't have. They can pick up small **electromagnetic** signals, which are small bits of electricity. Scientists think that hammerheads may be better at detecting electricity than other sharks because of their wide heads.

**1**

Start with a tilted oval. Add a curving triangle for the tail, and a pointed end for the head.

**2**

Look at the curved line in the tail fin. Draw it. Now look at the angle of the head. Draw it carefully, paying attention to angles.

**3**

Add the one eye you can see from this angle. Draw gill openings. Next add the pectoral and dorsal fins.

**4**

Add the pelvic, second dorsal, and anal fins.

**5**

Darken important lines and details. Add shading. Clean up by erasing any smudges or lines you no longer need.

# Whale Shark

The whale shark is the largest fish in the world. Whale sharks can be 50 feet (15.2 m) long and can weigh more than 30,000 pounds (13.6 tonnes). Whale sharks only eat small animals, such as shrimp and **plankton,** that they get by sifting water. The whale shark's mouth is more than four feet (1.2 m) wide. It draws water into its mouth and pushes it out of its **gills**. On the way, a special comb-like structure **filters** out larger animals. The whale shark is as big as a school bus, but it can only eat small animals because it has a tiny throat. It will choke if it tries to eat anything too big. Sometimes big tuna fish swim inside a whale shark's mouth and dine on the smaller fish there.

**1**

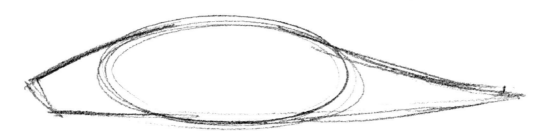

Draw a long, flat oval. Add a slanted box at one end for the head. Draw a long triangle at the other end for the tail.

**2**

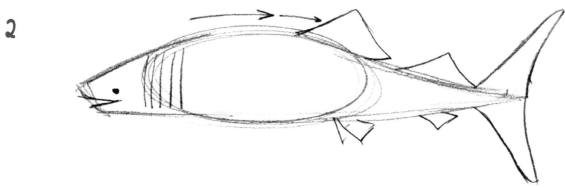

Draw the dorsal fins at the back of the whale shark's body. Add large gill openings. Draw the pelvic, anal, and tail fins. Add the mouth and an eye.

**3**

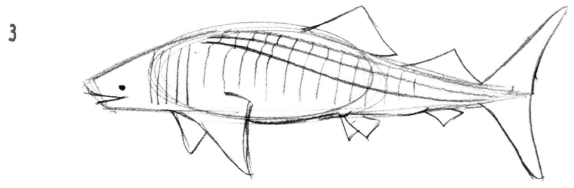

Next draw long ridges curving down the side and back of the shark's body. Add pectoral fins.

**4**

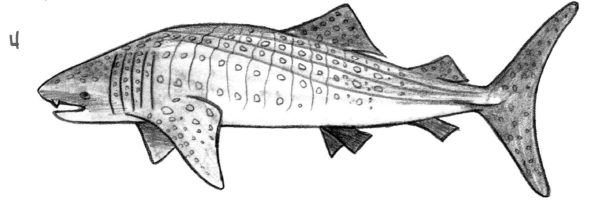

Add shading and patterns. Erase smudges and leftover lines.

# Basking Shark

The basking shark is the world's second-biggest shark. It can grow to 40 feet (12.2 m) long and weigh more than 8,500 pounds (3.9 tonnes). It eats small shrimp and plankton just as the whale shark does. It swims through the water with its mouth open. Up to 2,000 tuns (1,908 kl) of water pass through a basking shark's mouth every hour. These sharks eat a lot of food. One shark that was caught had over 1 ton (1 tonne) of food in its stomach. This shark got its name because it floats or basks on the surface of the ocean with its big dorsal fin in the air like a sail. The basking shark has been hunted for a long time. People in China and Japan make soup from its fins.

**1**

Draw a flat oval. Draw a square box at one end, and a triangle at the other. A backward 'S' curve forms the head.

**2**

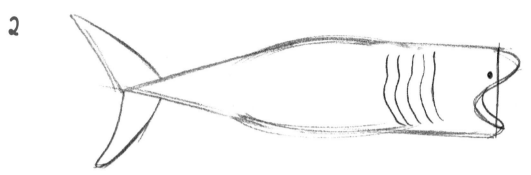

Draw the eye and open mouth. Draw very large gill openings. Draw the tail fin. Erase parts of the oval that you no longer need.

**3**

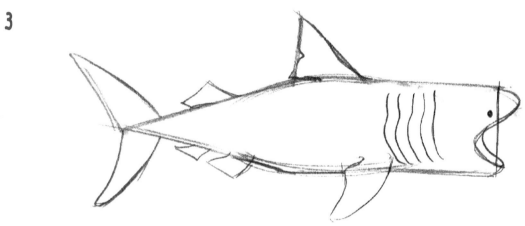

Put the dorsal fin above the middle of the oval. Draw the pectoral and remaining fins.

**4**

Finally, add shading and sharpen details. Clean up any smudges.

# Port Jackson Shark

The Port Jackson shark is named after a small port in Australia where it was first discovered in the late 1700s. This odd-looking shark has sharp spines in front of its dorsal fins. Port Jackson sharks are small, about five feet (1.5 m) long. They eat at night and feed on sea urchins and little shellfish. Port Jacksons are **migratory** sharks, which means they travel to different places at different times of the year. They travel to special **breeding grounds** to have their pups. The breeding grounds are areas where big male sharks don't usually go, making it safer for the newborn sharks. Port Jackson sharks lay eggs, which are sometimes found in the rocks at the bottom of the ocean.

1

Draw a long, flat oval with a rat-like tail.
Add a slanting box shape for the head.

2

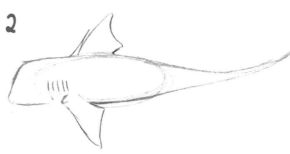

At the front of the oval, draw gill openings
and the pectoral fin. Add the dorsal fin, with
its pointed spine in the front.

3

Draw the eye high in the head. Draw the
mouth. Carefully add the tail fins.

4

Draw the second dorsal fin, and the fins on
the bottom.

5

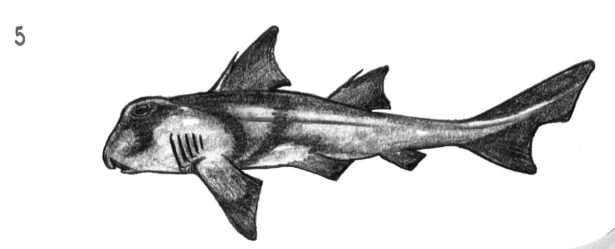

Add shading. Sharpen outlines and details. Clean up with your eraser.

21

# Drawing Terms

Here are some of the words and shapes that you will need to draw sharks:

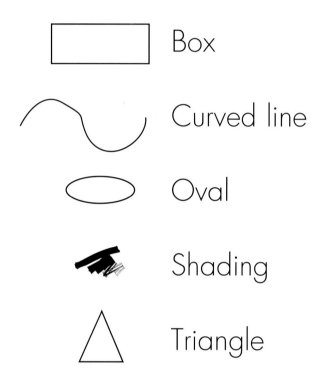

Box

Curved line

Oval

Shading

Triangle

# Glossary

**ancestors** (AN-ses-turz)  Relatives who lived long ago.

**breeding grounds** (BREED-ing GROWNDZ)  Places where a certain species of animal gives birth.

**class** (KLAS)  A group of animals with similar traits.

**electromagnetic** (ih-lek-troh-mag-NEH-tik)  Having a force of magnetism created by a small bit of electricity.

**endangered** (en-DAYN-jerd)  When something is in danger of no longer existing.

**evolve** (ee-VOLV)  To develop and change over many, many years.

**filters** (FIL-turz)  A process that removes larger objects from water or air.

**gills** (GILZ)  Organs that fish use for breathing.

**migratory** (MY-gruh-tor-ee)  When groups of animals move from one place to another.

**plankton** (PLANK-ten)  Tiny plants and animals that drift with water currents.

**predators** (PREH-duh-terz)  Animals that kill other animals for food.

**prey** (PRAY)  An animal that is hunted by other animals for food.

**rudder** (RUH-duhr)  A broad, flat, movable object that helps to steer something in water or air.

**species** (SPEE-sheez)  A single kind of plant or animal. For example, all people are one kind of species.

# Index

# Web Sites

To learn more about sharks, check out these Web sites:

http://www.seaworld.org/Sharks/classification.html
http://www.aqua.org